Create a Reward Plan for Your Child with Asperger Syndrome

★ John Smith

★ Jane Donlan

★ Bob Smith

Jessica Kingsley Publishers
London and Philadelphia

First published in 2008
by Jessica Kingsley Publishers
116 Pentonville Road
London N1 9JB, UK
and
400 Market Street, Suite 400
Philadelphia, PA 19106, USA

www.jkp.com

Library of Congress Cataloging in Publication Data
A CIP catalog record for this book is available from the Library of Congress

British Library Cataloguing in Publication Data
A CIP catalogue record for this book is available from the British Library

ISBN 978 1 84310 622 7

Printed and bound in Great Britain by
Athenaeum Press, Gateshead, Tyne and Wear

Contents

Chapter 1

Introduction

In November 2003 our son, Bob, was diagnosed with Asperger Syndrome (AS). He was eight years and nine months old at the time. During the time that has followed the diagnosis we have learned a lot about AS and have developed various techniques to help our son and to help us, as a family, to cope with the negative side of AS and to embrace its positive side.

So that you can put the information in this book into some sort of context we will say a little bit about ourselves and our lives.

Bob is our only child. At the time of writing Bob has been home-educated for approaching five years. He is now twelve. We parent Bob equally although we have been separated for about five years now.

Bob's dad is a mental health social worker. He spends most evenings and most of the weekend with Bob and we go on holidays together as a family. Bob lives with Mum, who is responsible for his day-to-day education. Bob's dad takes an active part in his education, taking him on lots of educational trips, and is mainly responsible for helping Bob with science.

We do all the usual family activities together and give Bob a full and happy family life.

Bob's AS has a really positive side. He is very bright and has an amazing sense of humour. He is very talented when it comes to writing poems and stories. Bob is a very loving child who loves to read and spend time with his dogs. He brings lots of fun and laughter into our lives.

Bob's AS also presents us with many challenges on a daily basis. However, we have learned that we all have to think about our behaviour and if necessary change it. It is not just Bob who has to change to fit in with us.

As you read through this book you will see how important it is to deal with conflict and challenge as a family and not just to blame the problems on the person with AS. It has become obvious to us that we all need to look at our behaviour and our responses to each other's behaviour in order to deal with conflict and challenge in an effective way.

The most effective tool we use to help us as a family to deal with the challenges AS brings is our **reward plan**. We decided to reward Bob's positive behaviour and not to punish his negative behaviour. We did this in a visual way by making a reward plan and awarding points for positive behaviour. Often reward plans award points, stars etc. for positive behaviour and then remove them for negative behaviour. We have learned that focussing on the positive is the best approach to use with a child with AS; in fact Bob thinks that this would be best for all children. It was his idea to put the reward plan in a book to help other children.

The reward plan helps to reinforce positive behaviours and is a great way of teaching Bob about appropriate behaviour in social situations, for example, how to make and keep friends. It has really helped to build Bob's confidence and helped him to cope with situations that he finds confusing such as queuing for a bus.

To supplement the reward plan we use some other techniques. These include:

★ **Scripts:** Written information to guide Bob through social situations. We have always written and drawn information for Bob since he was very young. We find this very effective.

★ **Signs:** These remind Bob about something we have agreed on. For example, his 'Shush' sign reminds him not to say 'Shut up' to Mum.

★ **Sketches:** These are drawings that we have used with Bob since he was little, long before his AS diagnosis. They are a visual way of passing on information, again usually about social situations or appropriate behaviour.

★ **Combining techniques:** We often use two or more of these techniques at the same time to reinforce information for Bob. Bob gets points for his reward chart when he uses/responds to these techniques.

We hope that you will be able to use our reward plan and our other techniques to help your family to get the best that you can out of AS. This book is meant as a practical aid to take some of the stress out of the daily challenges that you and your family may face when living with AS. In an ideal world people with AS would just be able to get on with their lives in their own honest way. Unfortunately the majority of people have little or no understanding or tolerance regarding difference and, as Bob often comes across as rude (to say the least!), a degree of social understanding and cooperation is really helping him to cope in a neurotypical world.

Chapter 2

What is Asperger Syndrome?

Before we start on how to create a reward plan, here is an informal overview of Asperger Syndrome (AS) and the effects it can have on those who have it. Knowing the kinds of difficulties that a person with AS may experience is really important when planning and using a reward plan because it will affect things like the kinds of achievements you decide to reward and the terms of the plan itself.

AS is part of the autistic spectrum of disorders. People with AS are said to be high-functioning, which means they are at the less severe end of the spectrum; however, people with AS can experience significant challenges with social and communication skills. Because people with AS usually have average or above average intelligence, AS can be very much a 'hidden disability' causing society on the whole to be less tolerant and accepting of these individuals.

It is important not to stereotype individuals with AS, so below is a list of symptoms that someone with AS *might* have.

The Triad of Impairments

Lorna Wing, an expert on autism, developed the theory of the Triad of Impairments – social and emotional impairment, language and communication impairment, and impairment in flexibility of thought.

Social and emotional impairment

People with AS often 'get it wrong' in social situations: this can range from letting the door slam in someone's face to making personal comments about someone's appearance. Bob will often say out loud the things that other people would only think. Here are some further examples of how AS affects Bob in practical terms.

EMPATHY AND SYMPATHY

People with AS may often feel empathy or sympathy but not know how to show it. They may not even recognize what they are feeling. Bob often shows a great deal of concern for people in developing countries when there is a drought, for holocaust victims, and particularly for animals that are suffering. It is harder for him to show empathy or sympathy on a more personal level. For example, if Mum hurts herself Bob will sometimes say 'Hah, good!', a totally inappropriate response! We feel that he knows a response is needed but doesn't know which one. On the other hand, if Bob has even the slightest bump he will immediately shout at Mum 'Show some concern! You're supposed to be my mother!' If Mum says 'Are you alright?' Bob will shout 'Don't be stupid! I wouldn't have said "Ow" if I was alright!' If it is a really minor incident and Mum ignores it Bob will shout 'RESPOND!' but whatever response Mum gives is always wrong! Recently we had a discussion about what Bob would like Mum to say in this situation. We have a tentative agreement on Mum saying 'Is it serious?'.

There is also a positive side to this kind of impairment. Bob is often able to see both sides of a situation because he is not immediately weighed down with an emotional response. This can be an advantage when having an intellectual discussion.

SOCIAL RULES

Bob has little understanding of social rules and etiquette and this leads to all sort of problems. He often 'gets it wrong' when we are out in public, for example, getting on the bus out of turn, or pushing past someone without saying 'excuse me'. Mum has been accused of being a 'bad mother' on a few occasions because Bob's lack of understanding comes across as bad manners.

Language and communication impairment

This can be anything from misinterpreting what someone says – for example, if someone uses a figure of speech such as 'This is the last straw', a person with AS might think 'Where? What straw?' – to not understanding facial expressions. Here are some examples of the ways in which this affects Bob.

BODY LANGUAGE

The non-verbal cues we use all the time, such as smiling or frowning and the way we stand or sit, all give cues to the people we interact with about how we are feeling. The 'reading' of non-verbal information usually develops naturally and is not consciously learned. It makes up the bulk of our communication. Children with AS probably won't develop these skills instinctively and may have to be taught in the way that other children are taught to read. It can take a long time for people with AS to learn to read facial expressions and body language and this makes social interaction extremely difficult for people with AS. Bob often has a 'blank' face and so it is hard for others to read how he is feeling by looking at him.

SPEECH

It can be hard for someone with AS to express emotion through speech as their intonation (tone of voice) is often flat and monotonous. For this reason, it is hard to gauge how Bob is feeling. Also, when responding to someone other than Mum or Dad Bob often looks away and mumbles. This works in reverse as well: people with AS may have difficulty detecting what other people express through their tone of voice, for example sarcasm or sympathy. Although Bob has a very good sense of humour and is always making jokes and making up silly scenarios he really struggles with sarcasm and gets very confused by it. He often struggles to understand jokes made by other people.

BEING PEDANTIC

Bob is incredibly pedantic. He is constantly correcting our grammar or factual information and often misses the general point of the conversation because he is so concerned with detail.

BEING LITERAL

A person with AS may take sayings or idioms such as 'I laughed my socks off' literally. But Bob can usually tell when something is a figure of speech and is more likely to take everyday conversation literally; for example, when he was younger 'just a minute' literally had to mean sixty seconds.

Sometimes, though, Bob will take things literally deliberately, just to make us laugh. Once Mum said to him 'Put everything off the sofa into your bedroom', meaning the books and comics and so on, and Bob put the dog in his room as well!

Being too literal can cause confusion for someone with AS. For example, if Mum says 'Bob, will you get the washing in?', Bob will simply say 'no'. If Mum says 'Bob, can you get the washing in?', Bob will say 'Yes I can' but won't actually do it. Mum would have to say 'Bob, get the washing in please' to achieve the desired effect.

CONVERSATION

Bob struggles with the concept of conversation. People with AS often have a special interest that they can become extremely knowledgeable about, often talking on and on about it and not noticing the listener's non-verbal cues that suggest he or she has heard enough (losing eye contact, looking around the room, looking at a watch). People with AS may also enjoy collecting things, which can go along with their special interests. Bob has collected everything from wrappers to dead insects over the years but his latest craze is Doctor Who. Collections and special interests can often dominate the conversation.

At other times, Bob will insist that Mum 'has a conversation' with him and gets annoyed if Mum doesn't think of an interesting subject in two seconds flat. Bob doesn't understand that you can't force someone to have a conversation, but that it should flow naturally. With the support of his speech therapist, Bob has recently made some cards with topics of conversation on that are interesting to him. He can carry these cards about with him. They are playing-card-sized and laminated. They help Bob to choose something he would like to talk about which takes away from Mum some of the pressure to think of a topic of conversation when she is thinking about other things, such as crossing the road. We call them 'Conversation Cards'.

Impairment in flexibility of thought

It is said that people with AS have difficulty seeing things from another's point of view and Bob certainly does have this rigid or inflexible thinking, especially on a personal level. An example of this would be when Mum and Bob are out and have agreed to go to a bookshop for Bob to look around, and we've said we'll do this next; if Mum then needs to find a toilet Bob will refuse because we said we were going to the bookshop next and the toilet wasn't 'in the agreement'.

Children with AS are thought to struggle also with imaginary, pretend games. Bob can play these games to a certain extent, for example, he would be happy with a scenario such as 'You be Harry Potter and I'll be Lord Voldemort'. If he knows who is doing what in a game he is okay for a while. However, he struggles when friends move on to another imaginary game too quickly. He then gets frustrated and this can lead to conflict.

ROUTINE AND CHANGE

Any sort of change, from something as massive as moving house to something as seemingly small as having a different brand of cheese, can be challenging for someone with AS. When Bob was younger his dragons had to be lined up exactly. If Mum moved them for dusting and misplaced one, even facing it left instead of right, Bob would have a major outburst.

Routine probably makes sense of the world to someone with AS, as it does with all of us. The difference is in the degree to which routine is important and the distress that can be caused by a change in routine for someone with AS.

Routine is very important to Bob. He can often be heard saying things like 'I don't do that now. I'll do it later, at the agreed time.' This could be about having a shower earlier than arranged or refusing to go to bed at 8.29 pm because bedtime is

8.30 pm. This is where Bob's reward plan comes in really useful (see the section on the Bedtime Plan in Chapter 6). Bob gets points for being flexible and changing his routine. For example, for months Bob would only have a bath on a Sunday from 7.15 to 7.45 pm so he could listen to Radio 4's children's programme *Go4It* in the bath. Using the reward plan to encourage flexiblility, Bob now listens to *Go4It* in his room and has showers at various times of the day throughout the week and even in the mornings!

Routine is probably so important to people with AS because it makes life less confusing. Unfortunately, society will not accommodate over-rigid routine and people with AS need to learn a degree of flexibility to 'get by' in a neurotypical world.

Other characteristics

That was the Triad of Impairments. Below are a couple of other characteristics that are also associated with AS.

Average or above-average intelligence

Bob is very intelligent and prides himself on this. From about the age of five he has dictated letters for us to send to our local member of parliament or the Prime Minister on issues he feels strongly about. He has a wide vocabulary for his age and often makes up his own words, such as 'disgustable' for something that is a mixture of 'horrible' and 'disgusting'. He has a flair for writing stories and poems.

When Bob was about eighteen months old Mum was looking through a book with him and pointing to objects and Bob was saying their names, such as 'boat', 'cat', and so on. Mum pointed to a bird and expected Bob to say 'bird'. He said 'kingfisher'. It was indeed a kingfisher. Mum said 'Cleverclogs, is there anything you don't know?' and Bob replied 'I don't know what clogs is'. He displayed two symptoms of AS on that occasion, above-average intelligence and taking things literally.

Sensory sensitivity

People with autism in general can often be sensitive to sight, sound, touch, taste and smell. This could form the subject for a whole book. Bob often gets overwhelmed by noise, especially if there are a lot of people around. He also finds it difficult to wear new clothes, and to touch certain fabrics. He often notices tiny things that would pass other people by, such as a faint smell or noise that no one else can hear. Recently, while sitting at the computer with Mum, Bob became very agitated because of a noise that Mum was making and he couldn't concentrate on what he was doing. The noise was just Mum's foot moving slightly against her sandal and was barely audible but he could hear it above everything else and it led to a small outburst.

Positive aspects

AS can present a lot of challenges for Bob but he also sees a positive side to having it. For instance, he has what he calls his 'Imaginings'. This is where he plays games in his head and makes up stories. At the same time he makes noises and has a lot of physical tics involving rigid arm and leg movements and facial grimaces. This is something Bob has always done though it has progressed over the years to include the leg movements and noises.

Bob's 'Imaginings' show a very creative side to Bob. He has, in recent years, been able to articulate what these 'Imaginings' are and what they mean to him. Some of the stories and games are very well thought out and the characters very detailed.

'Imaginings' are very important to Bob. He has to do them. He can hold them off for a period of time, for example when playing with a friend, but he has to 'release' them soon after. This often involves holding his breath and some very intense clenching of facial, hand, arm and leg muscles and occasionally he will hurt himself but on the whole his 'Imaginings' are beneficial for Bob and he is glad he has AS so that he can do them.

A final word

The purpose of this book is not to change your child and mould him or her into a neurotypical person, but to help them to 'get by' in a neurotypical world, while at the same time, we hope, embracing the beauty of AS – the intelligence, the honesty, the creativity, the loyalty. And, for parents, there is the joy of having a child who doesn't care which training shoes he wears because he doesn't notice which training shoes other children are wearing!

Bob's comments on AS

I think having AS is good but of course there are some parts of it that are bad.

What I like about having AS

I like my 'Imaginings' which are, as well as what I am seeing in front of me I can also see whole images inside my head. It's sort of like a cartoon going on inside my head. I don't just do them once. If I have a story I'll keep doing it until it comes to an end and sometimes it can have several endings and this can take weeks or years to finish, for example, there is one where there is this big sort of a company floating in the sky and held up by gas propellers. It's a fight between the guys who are in charge who are really evil and the guests who are invited on it before it goes up in the sky.

Sometimes I have 'Imaginings' that I only do in a particular place such as when I'm in Ibiza. I 'imagine' about different Samurai who have powers of different elements. There is a war going on between the Lightning and Ice on one side, Earth, Air, Wind and Fire on another.

Also, if I have a particular character that I like I may re-use it. One in particular has appeared in several of my 'Imaginings' including in both of the above examples. The character's appearance can change slightly over time, for example, he may have a different style of hair or wear glasses.

I don't just do this when I am walking about. I sit or stand in a particular position and clench my arms, hands and fingers and tense or jerk my legs. This position varies over time. Sometimes I put in little sound effects by making little noises and Mum thinks I'm holding my breath but I'm not. Also, sometimes, if I'm not happy with a character I change little parts of it; for example, I may give it a scar.

When I saw the Van Helsing film I began by acting out a kind of sequel to the film with my dogs where I was Van Helsing and they were monsters. I then put this into an 'Imagining'. If doing this technique I would advise you to only act out a few seconds of it otherwise it's hard to remember and do an 'Imagining' at the same time.

My 'Imaginings' are hard for other people to understand. When I used to go to school my teacher thought I was having an epileptic seizure when I was doing my 'Imaginings'. I wouldn't advise doing an 'Imagining' in public or at a friend's house unless they know about your autism. I used to but then I sort of realized it was a bad idea because I might get teased.

I have never met anyone else who does 'Imaginings' or similar things but with a different name. When I am reading a book sometimes I stop reading to put a particular action scene in to my 'Imaginings' before going back to the book. When I am watching something exciting on TV I am stimulated to do an 'Imagining' even though it has nothing to do with what is on TV. Music also makes me want to do 'Imaginings' instead of singing along to it. Also 'Imaginings' are good 'cos you can invent new words for scientific procedures when you don't know the word for it.

I also like having AS because it makes me intelligent and very good at making up stories and poems.

What I dislike about having AS

I find it hard to fit in with social etiquette, for example, getting on buses. I think it should just be whoever gets on first gets on first as opposed to queuing. Also, if someone is pregnant, they have specially reserved seats anyway so it doesn't matter when they get on. And also stuff like having to eat in a particular way when you go out to a restaurant. You should just be able to eat the way you eat. People shouldn't judge you on what you can and can't do. People should embrace more logical rules rather than 'if people do this in a particular way we should look down on them'.

I also don't like getting angry and irritated a lot and shouting.

Some of my opinions

Children should have their own branch of government because adults are more restricted by public opinion in thinking they need to fit in with the laws of society. I'm not saying all children aren't like that 'cos I know a lot are but of course there are some that think more like me and would make much better politicians than the ones we've got today, starting wars everywhere!

I think that people should stop being so obsessed with their appearance and care more about people's characters and that people should stop saying that we shouldn't discriminate against people who are disabled and people who have got a scar while they are still discriminating against people who look a little bit untidy or who are a bit dirty.

I think we should ban magazines that are all about celebrities, who really cares? We should get rid of the royal family, they don't do anything anyway and their ancestors were just a bunch of barbarians and murderers.

Prime Ministers or Presidents who start or support wars should be sacked. They are just warmongers!

We should really crack down on animal cruelty and start giving life sentences for killing animals.

I also think that they should start teaching about drugs and criminal activity in schools at a much younger age. I think that schools should care more about what children know rather than just what they can put down on paper and if they don't know anything, just teach them!

Society should start respecting children as equal to adults because we are. Children ought to be able to vote at the age of ten because if they were any younger they could be influenced and the BNP [British Nationalist Party] should be disbanded because they have racist views and it would be extremely dangerous if they came to power.

I hope this book is useful to you but if not don't blame me!

Chapter 3

Making a Reward Plan

Our reward plan is similiar to other reward plans you may have heard of. Your child receives points for positive behaviour, for example, practising something they find hard to do, such as a particular social skill. An agreed number of points will equal a reward for your child, thus reinforcing their positive behaviour.

Where our plan differs is that we are very specific about the wording used to describe what points are awarded for, and the plan is personalized for a particular child. Also, there is no assumption that the child knows about appropriate behaviour and chooses to ignore it, which parents of non-autistic children may assume about their child. A recent example of this concerned respect. Mum was very cross with Bob about the way he was speaking to her and said she wanted him to respect her. Bob insisted that he didn't respect Mum, that he loved her but didn't respect her. After a brief discussion about respect it soon became apparent that Bob didn't understand the full meaning of the word respect: he thought you could only respect people who had achieved great things and he pointed out to Mum that she hadn't achieved anything. We read the dictionary definition and talked about respecting people's feelings and their dignity. Bob seems to have a clearer idea about respect now but this is a good example of ensuring that your child knows what you mean and not making assumptions.

You must ensure that your child knows what you mean by appropriate, nice, acceptable, desirable behaviour. Because some children with Asperger Syndrome (AS) have average to above-average intelligence, we as parents can assume too much. Intelligence often masks the level to which your child may be struggling with something.

Remember, we are not trying to cure AS or give the child a personality transplant. We are simply trying to help the child cope with certain emotional responses, fears and actions that can have a negative effect upon the child and surrounding people. Also, we do not believe that society is going to change to suit a child with AS so we are trying to help the child to learn how to 'get by', at least, in a neurotypical world and, we hope, to enjoy it.

This reward plan, along with the other techniques we are using, should help you, as the child's significant adult, to examine, assess and if necessary change your own emotional responses and reactions to your child. *This is just as important as the changes you expect your child to make.*

Positivity

The reward plan is based on positivity. Only positive comments can be written on the reward chart. Your child receives points for positive behaviour and not for not displaying negative behaviour. This may sound confusing but the wording of what your child is given points for is very important.

For example, we would not write on Bob's reward plan 'I have points because I didn't hit Mum today'. This is very negative and acts as a reminder to Bob that he hits Mum sometimes and needs a reward plan to help him stop. It could evoke feelings of guilt, embarrassment and shame. (Also, Bob should not be hitting Mum and so should not be rewarded for not doing it.) If, however, we write 'I have points because I was calm and gentle with Mum today', this is positive and, we hope, leaves Bob feeling pleased and proud of his calm behaviour.

The hardest part for us in doing the reward plan was staying positive when the situation around us was feeling chaotic and out of control. For example, if Bob had had an outburst and had been hitting Mum, maybe biting, scratching, kicking, screaming and damaging the house, we found it terribly hard to pull anything positive out of the situation – but we have to. We often found ourselves scraping the barrel of our emotions to find something positive to say about Bob after such an experience. It would be something like 'I have points because I calmed down quickly after an outburst' or 'I have points because I said sorry to Mum after an outburst' or 'I have points because I tried to understand that saying sorry after an outburst is good if I wait a while until Mum is ready to hear sorry' or 'I have points because after an outburst I realized how much I had hurt Mum's feelings. It is good that I was aware that Mum was sad.'

We know that the temptation to punish for extreme aggressive or challenging behaviour can be overwhelming and that it makes more sense to do that than what we are saying but, to a child who is already filled with negative feelings, it would be like throwing petrol onto a bonfire.

Of course, when you and your child are calm, it is important to talk to your child about what happened and how it left people feeling. It's also worthwhile to talk about how you could deal with it better next time. This is where some of our other techniques can help in supporting the reward plan (see Chapter 4).

Please note: Where aggression and violence are concerned your child needs to be left in no doubt that these behaviours will not be tolerated. If you are experiencing aggression and violence then our strategies may help, but they should not be used in isolation. Seek professional help.

Back to the reward plan.

Specificity

The more specific you can be when writing achievements on the points chart, the easier it will be for your child to understand what the points are for and what is expected of him or her.

Consider the statement 'I have points because I was helpful'. This is vague and therefore may not encourage the helpful behaviour in the future. It would be far better to say 'I have points because I took the dishes into the kitchen when Dad asked me to'. This is specific and clear and may encourage your child to take the dishes into the kitchen without being asked. (It did in Bob's case.) Then you would write on the reward plan 'I took the dishes into the kitchen without being asked'.

Eventually you can phase out giving points for specific behaviours as they become second nature to your child. You can always reintroduce points if the required behaviour disappears again.

Giving points

★ **Points can only be given and can NEVER be taken away.** When you give your child points it is because your child has earned them. You have no right to take them away. Imagine an employer taking away the money you earned yesterday because they didn't like the work you were doing today! You would be outraged and rightly so. Well, so will your child if you take away points that he or she has already earned.

★ **Never use the reward plan as a temptation or a threat.** By 'temptation' we mean, for example, saying 'If you share your sweets you can have some points', or 'If you go to bed nicely you can have some points'. If you use the plan in this way you will find yourself arguing with your child over the reward plan because it has become a tool of manipulation. You would also be trying to force something onto your child that he or she is not ready for – in other words, setting your child up to fail. It is better to talk about the behaviours you would like to see more of and lead by example. By 'threatening' we mean forcing your child into behaving in a certain way by threatening to withhold or withdraw points. For example, don't say 'Right, no tidying up, no points!' or

'If you do that one more time you'll get no points!'

★ **Points are precious. They are earned. They are positive and used correctly they will raise your child's self-esteem.** We have made some of the mistakes we have described. You will too. Try not to make them too often and try to get back on track as quickly as possible.

Probably the hardest thing you will find about adjusting your child's behaviour is, as we have emphasised, adjusting your own and that of other important people in your child's life. Bob is an only child, but you may have other children's needs to consider when using the reward plan. Bob thinks it could be used for all children, and that is certainly something to consider if you have more than one child.

Should you involve your child's school in the reward plan?

As we home-educate Bob we are solely responsible for his reward plan. As most children go to school you may decide to share the awarding of points with your child's teacher. Without intending any disrespect of teachers, we would advise against this.

The reward plan needs to be carried out very carefully and positively. Teachers may be tempted to use points as temptations or gentle threats as they may not understand how crucial the wording of the reward plan is. Teachers are extremely busy people who have to care equally for maybe thirty children. They can't possibly take the time to carry out the awarding of points as carefully as you can. We know that you are very busy too but you have a lot more invested in your child than a teacher does.

We have seen teachers use a home/school diary in a very negative way, saying things like 'X has been silly today'. This is vague and negative. If you want to share the reward plan with your child's teacher (and some teachers would probably love to contribute) then you could ask the teacher to note your child's positive behaviours at school and you could then write them on your child's reward chart yourself, in your own words, and award points.

Reviewing the reward plan

For the reward plan to remain both effective for your child and workable for you, it is a good idea to review it regularly and make changes to it when appropriate. You might do this, for example, because certain behaviours have become habitual for your child, or because you need to adjust the number of points that are awarded for certain tasks so that they aren't too easy to achieve. If they were too easy, the reward plan might become boring for your child, not to mention expensive for you!

We started Bob's reward plan in the January two months after his diagnosis of AS. We reviewed the plan in the following September because Bob was doing so well. We decided to make it a bit more challenging for him. (See the original plan and revised plan later in this chapter.) We talked it through with Bob and showed him a copy of the new plan. We explained that we were making it more of a challenge because he was doing so brilliantly. He was so pleased with his progress and settled into the change quickly. As long as Bob is getting lots of rewards he doesn't care that much about the details.

Your child may respond differently to revising a reward plan, so take care. Don't rush into an updated plan. Introduce it slowly if you need to introduce it at all. If your child is unhappy maybe he or she is not ready for a review of the plan – you can always put it on hold.

We started the reward plan mainly to help with Bob's outbursts, which were extreme. Bob is a very gentle, loving and caring child but when he got overloaded emotionally it would come out as aggression, usually aimed at Mum or at objects in the house. Obviously this couldn't continue and, as we've already said, punishment just exacerbated things. There is no point in getting into an argument with a child with AS before he or she is ready to hear you. If you do you are just fuelling the fire.

We kept a chart of Bob's outbursts for a few months after we had started the reward plan and they reduced dramatically. Now, three years on, the worst thing Bob ever does is to nudge Mum with his elbow or push occasionally, and we are working on this as even this level of aggression is far from acceptable. However, Bob has made massive progress and we are very proud of how hard he has worked to reduce his outbursts. Bob's self-esteem was very low when he was having the outbursts because he disliked himself for hurting Mum. He is now a much happier and more confident child.

The single most effective thing we have done to help Bob with his outbursts is the reward plan. This is supported by our other techniques and help from professionals but if we could only choose one way to help Bob it would probably be the reward plan. We hope that one day Bob will be so well adjusted to the challenges that AS and the world throw at him that he won't need a reward plan, but at the moment we continue to use it to help Bob in all sorts of areas.

Number of points

So how many points do you award? That is up to you, but our advice is to keep it simple, maybe on a scale of one to ten. Children with AS often respond well to visual stimuli so you may want to draw your scale as, for example, a ladder or thermometer. You could draw a ladder with the steps numbered from one, the lowest, to ten, the highest, to explain your points system to your child. You could use your imagination and use a different visual scale if you want to.

Bob usually gets between one and four points for most things. He would get a ten if he managed to deal with an outburst in a safe way. He may get two for saying 'hello' and 'goodbye' to his grandparents unprompted. He would probably get a five for saying 'goodbye' unprompted when leaving a library or other public place, to someone he doesn't know well, say a librarian.

You must decide how many points you will award because only you know the areas in which you are trying to help your child, which take priority. For example, if your child is having outbursts like Bob did then you would probably be prioritizing that and maybe giving fewer points if your child takes the dishes into the kitchen, although still acknowledging this act of independence and helpfulness.

If you can, try to notice all the seemingly little things and give a point or points for them because they may not be so little to your child. To put clean clothes on would seem usual for a twelve-year-old who doesn't have AS but for many reasons it may seem like a momentous task to a child who does. You will know best when it comes to your child even if you don't think you will.

What to give points for

What might you give points for on the reward plan?

★ **Social and communication skills.** This covers a very wide area so here are a few examples:

☆ Saying 'hello' or 'goodbye' unprompted to someone your child knows well.

☆ Saying 'hello', 'goodbye', 'please' or 'thank you' to people your child comes across in public, for example, a shop assistant, bus driver or librarian.

☆ Playing cooperatively with a friend. This can be very hard for a child with AS if he or she has no concept of being wrong and really struggles to see another child's point of view. This was very much the case with Bob and still is to some extent. His friendship skills have been improved by giving him points for dealing with conflict calmly, for laughing and playing with a friend, for taking turns and more recently by rehearsing a question or two he might ask a friend to show an interest in them, for example, 'Did you have a nice birthday?' or practising an answer to a question a friend may ask, for example, 'Did you have a good holiday Bob?'. These skills can be practised (and rewarded) with a variety of people, not just friends.

☆ Starting conversations. Bob finds it really hard to instigate a conversation with his Dad and even to use the word 'Dad' despite the close bond they have. Bob is unable to explain why this is but he is practising starting a conversation with Dad and using the name 'Dad' and being rewarded for his efforts.

☆ Holding the door open for someone who is coming behind them. Bob often lets doors slam in people's faces though he is more aware since he has been practising and getting points for holding doors open.

★ **Helping around the house or garden.** This may initially be when asked but we hope will lead to more spontaneous activity, as with Bob taking the dishes into the kitchen. This will also increase your child's self-esteem and encourage their independence.

★ **Being flexible.** This is something your child may find really difficult to do. Give a point or points for what may seem to you to be a tiny amount of flexibility such as having brown bread instead of white and give more points for a large amount of flexibility such as coping well with a change of routine or change of plan at short notice. Bob receives a lot of points for being flexible as day-to-day living can be very restricted when you are forced to live by someone else's routines. It will also help to prepare your child for 'the big wide world' where other people are not going to have the same respect or patience that you may have for your child's routine and inflexibility.

★ **Calm behaviour.** Again this covers a wide area.

  ☆ You may want to give your child points for asking nicely for something instead of demanding it, as most people with AS don't realize when they're coming across as rude.

  ☆ It may be that your child is 'snappy' or short-tempered when they are anxious or overwhelmed and you want to help them to speak more politely to you.

  ☆ You may have more serious issues with your child such as the outbursts that Bob used to have. Picking up on any display of 'nice' behaviour and praising and rewarding this can only be a positive thing for your child and will really help with their confidence and self-esteem.

★ **Decision making.** Bob really struggles with making decisions. However small the decision, we try to acknowledge it and, if we remember, write it on his reward chart and give points.

★ **Acts of independence.** We try to encourage Bob's independence by making positive comments on his reward chart about it and giving him points. This can be anything from cleansing his own skin to going into a shop to buy something. Occasionally he will now do this if he doesn't have to ask for assistance in the shop but it took a lot of practise and points. It was a gradual process of going to the counter with Mum or Dad, then Mum or Dad being in the shop but not at the counter, then Mum or Dad waiting at the shop door, and so on. We are hoping that he will get to the stage of going into a shop and asking for help if he needs it but this may be some way off.

★ **Expressing emotions.** It can be hard for children with AS to express their emotions as it is often hard for them to recognize the emotions either that they feel themselves or that other people are feeling. If your child is able to tell you how he or she feels, or even attempts to tell you how he or she feels then this can be encouraged by giving points on the reward chart with a sentence of explanation. Sometimes when Bob was younger he would get angry because his face was wet. He wasn't aware of being upset and didn't even realize that he was crying. If your child shows any concern about other people's feelings this is to be encouraged. The expression and recognition of their own and other people's emotions/feelings can be a major obstacle to

> people with AS when developing relationships. Bob is more able to articulate his feelings since using the reward plan although it still takes him a long time to talk about his feelings, probably because he is still struggling to recognize them a lot of the time.

The above list is intended to give you an idea about the sort of things you may want to reward your child for but of course each child is different and will have different strengths, challenges and needs. Each of the above points could be broken down into many examples and be far more detailed because there is so much about the neurotypical world that is confusing and over-whelming to a child with AS. However, we hope this list has given you a starting point.

Rewards

In considering what to give as rewards, and how often, you will need to decide what is most suitable for your child and your budget. Rewards do not always have to cost money. They could be, for example, extra TV time or computer time, if this is appro-priate and not something you are trying to discourage. You could award an extra trip to the park or lots of choice time, where you spend time with your child doing what your child wants to do, within reason! We are not suggesting that your child has to earn time with you. You could award time where you agree to play, for example, a game that you hate. In our case it was the Pokémon card game, which we find boring and confusing.

Consult with your child. If they can 'cash in' points for a reward, what, realistically, would they like? Remember, this need not just be material rewards. Encourage and help your child to choose. Bob struggles greatly with choice and decision making. He has never even asked for a specific birthday or Christmas present.

We recommend rewards on a scale. For example, set a target to achieve a small reward. Originally ours was 50 points. A medium reward was 100 points. A big reward was 150 points (see our original reward plan later in the chapter). Don't be too ambitious with expensive rewards because once your child learns that appropriate behaviour equals points and points equal rewards, those points will soon build up!

If, as lots of children with AS do, your child has a special interest or interests (in Bob's case, reading, dragons, collecting anything from wrappers to dead insects) then this may be helpful when deciding on suitable rewards (though Bob would probably feel shortchanged if we gave him a dead insect as a reward!).

For the purpose of maintaining your child's health and well-being we don't advise using sweets/chocolate, fast-foods and so on as rewards too often. Also, using food as a reward or comfort can lead to an unhealthy attitude to food – 'I've worked hard so I deserve chocolate'. If your child does this too often, his or her health will be affected, though of course most of us do it sometimes!

Reward suggestions

Small rewards:

- ★ stickers

- ★ chocolate bar

- ★ a small amount of money to spend

- ★ comic

- ★ charity shop toy or book

- ★ colouring book or crayons

- ★ drawing pad and pencils.

Medium rewards:

- ★ toy

- ★ game

- ★ book

- ★ Top Trump cards

- ★ envelope with a small amount of money in

- ★ extra visit to the swimming pool/library/ another of your child's favourite places.

Big rewards:

- ★ books

- ★ audio book

- ★ music album

- ★ trip to the cinema, theatre or a concert

- ★ outing to a museum or gallery

- ★ a meal out

- ★ envelope with a surprise suggestion for an outing

- ★ envelope with an amount of money in.

Rewards that don't cost money:

- ★ extra time on the computer

- ★ time spent playing a game of choice

- ★ trip to the park

- ★ staying up a bit later

- ★ extra time to spend on your child's special interest, maybe sharing it with them.

Reward bag

As a week or a couple of weeks can seem a long time to a child who is saving up points for a reward we decided to also use a reward bag. If Bob was saving 150 points for a big reward but we wanted to acknowledge how well he was doing we would occasionally allow him to choose from the reward bag. We call it 'an immediate reward'. (If, like Bob, your child struggles with choice then you may need to limit it to two choices or just offer something of your choice.) Bob often chooses things for the reward bag and plans the order in which he wants to earn things.

We usually include comics, the odd chocolate bar, a small toy (charity shops can be really useful here). Sometimes we put something really special in just to spice things up and maintain Bob's interest. For Bob this may be a DVD/video, a story tape or CD, or a book he has been longing for. You will have to consider your budget and the needs of your other children, if you have more than one child, when rewarding your child with AS.

Personalizing your child's reward plan record sheets

We chose the design of a dragon as Bob collects dragons and has lots of toy and model ones. He has always loved dragons. Mum drew it but, if that worries you, you can always get your child to design the picture or use a photocopy of something your child really loves such as a pet. Your child may prefer no picture or a change of picture.

We use a new front page on the record sheets (with the dragon picture on) for each month. It means we can review each month separately. Blank examples of our record sheets are shown on pp.43 and 44. These templates are available for readers to download at www.jkp.com/catalogue/book.php/resources/9781843106227.

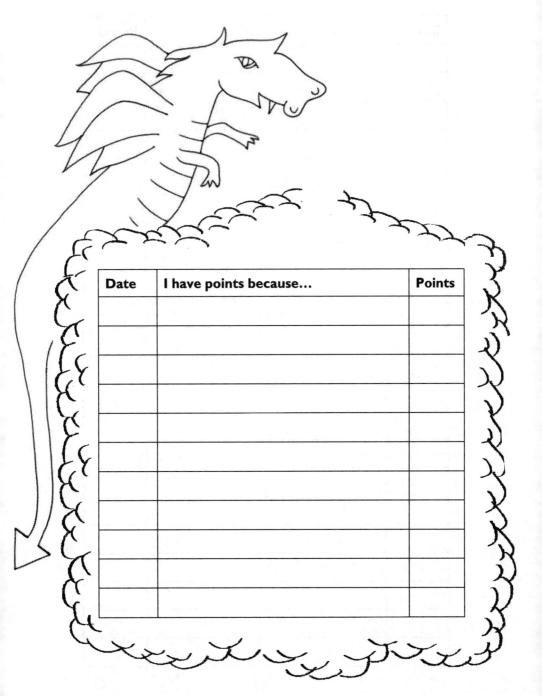

Date	I have points because…	Points

Front page of record sheet

Date	I have points because...	Points

Continuation of record sheet

Going over your child's points together

We go over the points that Bob has for each day about half an hour before bedtime. We read out what the points were for and how many points he has in his running total. This reinforces future desired behaviour and also gives a positive ending to the day.

Sometimes it's hard to remember at the end of the day all the things Bob deserves points for so we try to write them down throughout the day as well. Sometimes, if it is for something really subtle, like Bob looking up when someone is talking to him, it is easy to forget this at the end of a busy day but it is such an important thing that he deserves points for it.

Also, you may get 'reward plan fatigue', especially if you are writing all the points at the end of the day. Sometimes we just feel too tired and occasionally we do forget to read points out. In this case we read them out the next morning. You will get tired of keeping records and having to think all the time about the things you need to encourage or discourage in your child, especially when you see these things happening in a more natural way in your friends' children, but try to keep going. Our reward plan really is one of those things where the more you put into it the more you will get out of it.

Age

The reward plan could work for children of all ages. Bob was eight when we started the reward plan and we have revised it many times since then to suit his needs at particular times.

If you want to use the reward plan with a teenager then talk to them about it. See how they feel. They may be happy to try it if it means getting stuff they want. Explain that it can be kept confidential. We always keep Bob's reward plan out of sight when people come to the house because it is private.

So, to sum up ...

★ Design a cover that is attractive to your child.

★ Decide on a scale of points.

★ Decide how many points are needed to earn a reward.

★ Decide which behaviours you are trying to encourage/discourage. Which life skills are you trying to teach?

★ Make sure you're specific when writing down the behaviours you reward.

★ Remember that this is a process and you will not achieve all you wish to overnight. You may see some change very quickly if the plan works well for you.

★ Prioritize. You may have to prioritize skills and behaviours you wish to encourage/discourage. Don't expect too much too soon.

★ The most important thing is to keep the plan **positive**.

Make sure that the person with AS understands that all members of the family need to adapt their behaviour to suit each other. We are not trying to isolate the person with AS and change them to suit the family.

And finally, please don't force the reward plan on your child. If it is not welcome it won't work. Because children with autism and AS often appreciate visual information you may want to do a 'mock' reward plan when introducing the idea to your child, to show him or her how it would work and what sort of thing they might get points and rewards for.

Good luck! We hope that you and your child enjoy our reward plan and that it is as successful for you as it has been for us.

The original reward plan (begun in January)

When Bob behaves in a calm and respectful way he will be awarded a point or points. If Bob is kind, helpful or considerate, or compromises well, he will receive a point or points.

NICE BEHAVIOUR = POINTS

POINTS = REWARDS

50 points = One pound to spend in a charity shop,

or

An extra video from the library,

or

A new magazine.

100 points = A book to the value of five pounds,

or

A toy to the value of five pounds.

150 points = An extra meal out,

or

An extra trip to the theatre,

or

An extra trip to the cinema.

Bob can use up his points when he reaches 50 and then start again from 0, or keep saving points until he gets to 100 and use them then start again at 0, or save up all his points until he reaches 150 and get a bigger reward.

Points will be given for positive behaviour but points will NEVER be taken away for negative behaviour.

(This original reward plan focussed on calm and gentle behaviour, although points could be given for other things, because at that time Bob was having 'outbursts' almost daily and often hitting Mum and damaging things in the house. To be fair to Bob, he had been coping with undiagnosed AS for years and it's no wonder the frustrations built up. Now, three years on, we use the reward plan to help Bob with his social and communication skills, including being flexible, which is our main focus at present.)

The first revision to the reward plan (begun in the following September)

Bob responded so well to the original reward plan that, with Bob's agreement, we revised the plan to make it a bit more challenging for Bob.

100 points = Choose something from the reward bag.

250 points = A bigger reward, for example, cinema, theatre, meal out or a surprise that Mum or Dad buy; maybe a toy, book or story tape/CD.

Occasionally Mum or Dad will give a spontaneous reward for especially nice behaviour. (For example, on September 29th, Mum bought Bob the 'Beano Special' comic in recognition of his calm behaviour and for speaking nicely to Mum.)

Subsequent revisions to the reward plan

As we noted before, it's a good idea to modify the reward plan to prevent it from becoming too easy or too expensive. So, in the following March, we raised the lower points to 150. And in the following year, in January, we revised the points system again, to say

200 points = Something from the reward bag, for example a toy or book.

To be honest, we hadn't planned on using the reward plan for so long but as we achieve certain goals with Bob there are always new ones! As we have said, at the moment we are concentrating on Bob's social and communication skills and on his being flexible with his routine. So you see there is always something more to do and as long as the reward plan is working for Bob we will stick to it.

Bob's comments on the reward plan

The reward plan is a very good idea. It is a good idea because I 'get stuff!' I get points and this encourages me to do things that I find difficult such as staying calm or asking for something in a cafe. Points help me to stay calm and I feel good about myself when I am calm.

Chapter 4

Other Techniques to Supplement the Reward Plan

The reward plan is the most useful tool we use with Bob but we also use other tools, often in combination with the reward plan, to help Bob and ourselves to put the plan into action smoothly and successfully. The three tools we'll talk about here are scripts, sketches and signs, and each can be useful for different reasons:

★ Scripts, sketches and signs provide an alternative to verbal communication. Verbal communication can be difficult for children with Asperger Syndrome (AS), so we use other visual techniques instead to explain things.

★ Scripts and sketches are useful for reinforcing the aims of the reward plan by explaining clearly what we'd like Bob to aim towards.

★ Signs can help Bob, Mum and Dad to adopt preferred behaviours quickly and easily, with a minimum of upset.

Scripts

We have always written things down in a straightforward format or drawn things (see the section on sketches below) for Bob to explain things that he finds difficult. We did this long before his AS was diagnosed and continue to do it now. We use these scripts to simplify situations for Bob and to explain how his behaviour can impact on other people. They are a really useful way of reinforcing the social and communication skills he is trying to learn.

Despite Bob's high IQ, we find that the more simple the script the more effective it is. In the script we usually include:

★ a brief sentence saying what the script will be about

★ any feelings that need to be considered, our child's or someone else's

★ why we should or shouldn't do what ever the script is advising

★ a sentence saying how proud we/Bob will be if he achieves the aim of the script.

Once we've written a script, we might read it together with Bob, or Bob might read it himself as a reminder of the particular behavioural responses it describes. Below is an example of a script that we wrote to help Bob to understand that he cannot control other people's facial expressions.

Facial expressions

Sometimes, when I feel upset, agitated or overwhelmed I get cross if Mum has a particular expression on her face. Sometimes I will tell Mum to change her facial expression or tell Mum to stop glaring at me.

I am trying to learn that facial expressions are reflex reactions to certain feelings or moods. I am trying to learn that sometimes people cannot control their own facial expressions, especially if that person is upset or angry. The facial expression is a response to that person's feelings at that moment in time.

I could try to learn to use Mum's facial expressions to work out how Mum is feeling. I might need some help with this.

I am trying to learn that people look at each other when they communicate, even in anger. Sometimes I feel that Mum is glaring at me when she is angry. Mum will try not to glare.

Dad and Mum will help me to learn more about facial expressions.

Dad and Mum will be very pleased if I try to learn that I can't control people's facial expressions and I will be pleased with myself.

We wrote this script because Bob used to try to rearrange Mum's face if he thought that Mum was looking angry or upset. Sometimes he would use his hands and sometimes he would shout and order Mum to smile or not to look angry or upset. He seemed to think that if he could manipulate a smile onto Mum's face using his hands then Mum wouldn't be cross, say, because she would be smiling. Even now Bob still thinks that Mum is staring at him even if Mum is looking past him, for example, out of the window. However, he has more understanding about facial expressions being beyond his and sometimes Mum's control since we wrote the script.

Like the reward plan, our scripts try to make it clear that the onus isn't solely on Bob to change his behaviour and that Mum and Dad are prepared to change theirs as well. We ensure that when Bob does try to make positive changes he is awarded points accordingly.

Signs

These are simple visual representations of certain ideas made into a sign that Bob can carry with him and bring out when it's appropriate, either as a reminder to himself or as a request to others to do something. Again, they replace the need for spoken communication.

Signs are an effective and immediate way of helping your child and yourself to remember really important things, such as calming down. Sometimes, in the heat of the moment, it is easy to forget to be calm and to shout or nag at your child. If your child shows you a calming down sign it is a quick, visual reminder of the agreement you've made to avoid shouting, and of the preferred behaviour that is expected of you and your child.

We have designed, made and used signs for a variety of situations when trying to adapt our own and Bob's behaviour to accommodate AS. Sometimes we have written a script to go alongside the sign (see Chapter 5). We usually make the sign on a piece of card small enough to be able to take out with us if necessary. We used to put layers of sticky tape over the sign to strengthen it but now we use a laminator, which is much more effective.

Below are examples of signs and the reasons we made them.

The LET'S CALM DOWN! sign

This sign was made to help Bob to reduce his outbursts. Bob is a naturally gentle and loving person but when the negative side of AS took over Bob would lose control. To be fair to Bob most of these outbursts took place before his diagnosis of AS and for about six to twelve months after, when we were all still learning about AS and what it meant for us as a family.

It very quickly became apparent that our reactions to Bob's outbursts would have a huge impact on the severity of the outburst. If we shouted at Bob or tried to reprimand him in any way during an outburst then the outburst would get bigger and last longer. Bob only really had these outbursts with Mum and often Dad would have to be called to the house at midnight or later to calm Bob and Mum down as both would be sobbing for hours after one of Bob's outbursts. The problem was that although Mum had always been a very calm and patient person previously, Bob's birth had been a very violent one which left Mum with a lot of physical damage and years of operations, pain and so on. Also, Bob rarely slept and was in Mum's bed until he was nearly ten (you can see how we overcame this eventually with our Bedtime Plan in Chapter 6). So Mum was exhausted and responding inappropriately to Bob's outbursts, by shouting, crying, or both.

Bob and Mum designed the sign and made it. We wrote a script to accompany it. The important thing about this sign is that it needs to be shown as soon as you sense that you or your child are feeling even slightly angry. Too often we left it until

Mum shows this sign to Bob

Bob shows this sign to Mum

Calming down – script to accompany the sign

Sometimes I feel a little bit annoyed.

This feeling can very quickly grow into anger.

When I get angry I might say or do something that will make me unhappy with myself when I am calm.

If Mum shows me my 'Let's Calm Down' sign it might remind me to calm down before my anger gets too big.

If Mum starts to get angry I can show her her own 'Let's Calm Down' sign.

Together we can try to deal with angry feelings without upsetting each other.

Bob was visibly angry and then he would just snatch the sign and throw it across the room. It is hard to detect how your child is feeling when their facial expression doesn't give you any clues, but keep the sign in your pocket and observe your child closely, especially at times when you know from experience that your child may get stressed.

This particular sign took a long time to work but it did work with persistence, with re-reading the accompanying script on a regular basis and with Bob seeing the use of the signs as a big earner in terms of his reward plan! (We make sure that we always reward Bob when he uses signs appropriately.)

The SHUSH! sign

Bob often feels that he needs Mum to stop talking. He gets very stressed if Mum is talking when he needs quiet. Bob used to shout at Mum to 'shut up'. As with many people on the autism spectrum, over-stimulation such as too much noise can be difficult for Bob to deal with, but being told to shut up was demeaning for Mum and embarrassing when out in public! The worst thing was that Mum then found it difficult to stay calm as well because she'd been told to shut up, so she might say something stupid like 'No, you shut up'. Comments like these are futile. Bob's senses are overwhelmed at this point so the last thing he needs is more noise. Besides Mum has said something that Bob has been asked not to say!

We wrote a script to help Bob to stop telling Mum to shut up and to ask her to be quiet nicely and discreetly, and we also made a sign. Mum promised to take her own advice and try not to get cross with Bob when he asked her to be quiet.

The agreement was that when Bob wanted Mum to stop talking he would show Mum the sign or put his finger gently to his lips. It took a bit of practice and lots of reminders, including re-reading the accompanying script and also lots of points for the reward plan for using the sign. Eventually Bob did remember to use the sign. If he is feeling particularly anxious

The SHUSH! sign

then he still sometimes resorts to saying 'shut up' to Mum but not very often.

One day we were on the bus and didn't have the shush sign with us. Bob said to Mum 'Mum, will you please be quiet, you are talking too much'. Although the woman sitting behind us probably thought this sounded rude and Mum was still a bit embarrassed, we thought Bob did a great job and gave him points for it.

The DAD WILL BE COMING LATER sign

Bob has always been very anxious when waiting for Dad to come to the house. He asks in the morning and continues to ask all day long 'What time is Dad coming?', 'How long until Dad comes?'. It got to the point where Bob was saying he didn't want Dad to come every night. We knew that Bob loved Dad and was always happy to see him so we couldn't understand why Bob kept saying this.

We established (after a few years!) the reason for it. Bob hates uncertainty. He needs to know what is happening and when and not knowing the exact time that Dad would arrive each night was causing him great anxiety. He just wanted a break from feeling so anxious, so if he knew for sure that Dad wasn't coming then he needn't feel so anxious all day. It is so obvious with hindsight but it took years for Bob to be able to articulate this to us and in the meantime Dad was feeling upset that Bob didn't want to see him every day!

To help Bob to reduce this anxiety we talked to him about things he could do, for example, talk to Mum if he started to recognize anxious or uncomfortable feelings when waiting for Dad. We wrote a script and also made a sign. We were already using a 'later' sign that Bob's speech therapist had given us so

Bob developed this into a 'Dad will be coming later' sign. He did a picture of Dad driving home from work. If Bob starts to ask when Dad is coming and he or Mum detect any anxiety in Bob then Mum gives Bob the sign to hold. It is a reminder that Dad is coming but we don't know exactly what time.

This sign has significantly reduced Bob's anxiety in waiting for Dad and of course he gets points on his reward plan for using it. This sign was effective immediately.

The DAD WILL BE COMING LATER sign

Sketches

Along with scripts, sketches are something we have used for a long time with Bob, long before his diagnosis of AS, when we were struggling on our own to find ways to help with his outbursts in particular.

Sketches are a really simple and useful way of offering your child a visual explanation of an idea or scenario. Sketches have really helped us to get information over to Bob ever since he was very young. Below are some examples of sketches and explanations of why we needed them.

The DEALING WITH CONFLICT sketch

In this situation Bob was becoming very frustrated by the behaviour of his 'friend' Harry. Harry had learned, from Bob's reactions, that sticks were very important to Bob. If Harry took a stick from Bob and held it too high for Bob to reach then Bob would end up crying, shouting and eventually chasing Harry and threatening to kill him.

Bob prides himself on his intellect so we tried to explain that he needed to use his brain to deal with Harry. We asked Bob to choose names for the two characters we planned to use for the sketch. He named them Fatso and Chewey. We then explained to Bob that Fatso was giving her power to Chewey by allowing Chewey to control her behaviour (see the Fatso and Chewey sketch on p.62).

After Bob had grasped this concept we then did drawings of Bob and Harry and asked Bob how he could 'out-smart' Harry in the future. Bob said he would find a stick that he didn't care about but he would pretend he did care about it. He would wait for Harry to take it. Bob would then 'act casual' and Harry would learn not to take sticks from Bob because there was no longer any reward in it for him. Bob called this 'psychological warfare'.

This was a brilliant idea and it did work for a while. Unfortunately Harry learned other ways to wind Bob up and we ended up keeping Bob away from Harry for a while until he had learned more skills and had more confidence in controlling his anger and frustration. These days Bob and Harry just keep out of each other's way when we all meet up with mutual friends. We call this progress!

Dealing with conflict

Chewey insults Fatso.

What might Fatso do?

    Fatso might whack Chewey over the head.

What might happen to Fatso if she does?

    Fatso might get into trouble.

How might Chewey feel if Fatso gets into trouble?

    Chewey might feel powerful because she caused Fatso to get into trouble. She might feel happy.

Chewey insults Fatso.

If Fatso ignores Chewey what might happen?

Chewey keeps calling names.

Fatso keeps ignoring.

Chewey stops calling names.

Fatso has kept her dignity and feels good about herself.

Chewey learns that she doesn't have the power to upset Fatso.

Dealing with conflict

Bob has a stick.

Harry takes Bob's stick.

He holds it high so Bob can't get it back.

What can Bob do?
    Bob could punch Harry.

What might happen to Bob then?
    Bob would get into trouble.
    Harry might punch Bob back.
    Harry could still have the stick.
    Harry would learn how to upset Bob – by taking the stick.

What else could Bob do?
    Not get sticks when Harry's around.
    Ask an adult for help.

Wait a few minutes then ask Harry for it back.

Ignore Harry – don't let him see how upset Bob is.

What must Bob not do?

Hit Harry.

Push or pull Harry.

Scratch or bite Harry.

Make threats.

Shout or scream.

Hurt Harry in any way.

We were very strict about this at the time because Bob got so distressed about this he could have taken things too far.

The OTHER PEOPLE CAN'T READ MY MIND sketch

Another sketch which worked particularly well for Bob was one about other people not being able to read his mind. If you have a child with AS you will probably have experienced this. Bob always struggled with the idea that his thoughts are private. He always assumed that if he knew something then everyone else would know it too.

This covers lots of situations. Bob's catch phrase could be 'Isn't it obvious?' because he says this to us all the time. An example is when Bob hurts himself and we are not aware of it (he may be in a different room). He will come in to us and say 'I said Ow!' When we ask why, he will say 'Well isn't it obvious?' If we ask where and how he got hurt we get the same reply. He assumes that because he knows we should know. The sketch helped with this somewhat. He still assumes we have the same information he has but not as often and he did show a good understanding of the idea that other people can't read his mind when we used the sketch to explain it.

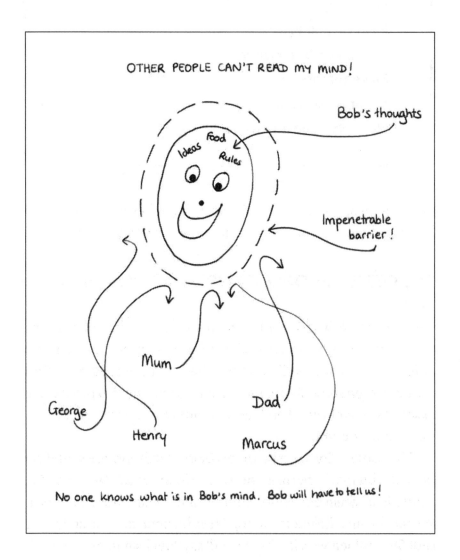

Bob's comments on the supplementary techniques

I found the signs helpful. They all helped. The 'shush' sign and the 'later' sign were the most helpful.

The 'shush' sign helped me to stop getting into trouble for telling Mum to 'shut up' and the 'later' sign helped me to feel less anxious about waiting for Dad to come.

I came up with the idea of a dog-shaped sign to help me stop shouting in front of my dogs Fred and Fido.

The sketches are very useful and helpful. End of story!

Chapter 5

Combining Techniques

We use lots of different techniques to help Bob to cope with the challenges that Asperger Syndrome (AS) can sometimes throw at him. As we've said, the techniques we use regularly are the reward plan, scripts, sketches and signs. Each of these techniques can be used in isolation but often we find that we get better results by combining two or more of them.

One example of this is what we did to help Bob deal with conflict appropriately. We started by drawing a sketch and writing a script to address the difficulty of dealing with situations of conflict. We also used the 'Let's Calm Down' sign in practice, if Bob began to get upset and, of course, if Bob responded to the sign he would get points on his reward chart for behaving well in a difficult situation. Combining all four techniques in this way helped us to achieve a positive outcome.

Dealing with conflict – script

Sometimes I get cross with my friends.

If they break the rules of a game or change the rules of a game I feel upset with them.

I can sort this out by talking to my friends or asking a grown-up for help.

Sometimes I may have to accept that my friends and I disagree. If I insist on being proved right my friends may fall out with me.

I must not shout at my friends or use any physical means (such as shoving, grabbing, or pushing).

I must deal with conflict calmly.

If I deal with conflict calmly my friends may repect me.

If I deal with conflict calmly Dad and Mum will be very pleased with me.

I will be pleased with myself.

Dealing with conflict calmly – sketch

Game Changes

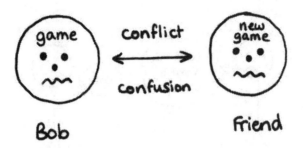

This is what usually happens

This is what could happen

Or

Sometimes arguments over a game may not be sorted out and children may have to play a different game.

Combining techniques has been very useful for our family. Remember, you may have to return to scripts or sketches to remind your child of what they have learned. We advise rewarding your child with points when they have responded well to a script, sketch or sign.

Chapter 6

Specific Reward Plans

We have done two specific reward plans to help with big changes for Bob:

★ the Bedtime Plan

★ the 'Caring for myself tasks' Plan.

The Bedtime Plan

This plan was developed to get Bob out of Mum's bed and sleeping in his own bed. Bob had slept with Mum from being a toddler and the Bedtime Plan was started when he was nine, nearly ten.

Bob has always had trouble getting to sleep and would often not want to be upstairs by himself. As a result Mum was going to bed early nearly every night but not actually going to sleep. Sometimes Bob would mess about, always he would talk (and talk!) and Mum was becoming more and more exhausted. Bob also got out of bed repeatedly to go to the bathroom. Mum would eventually get cross and lose patience with Bob, and Bob would have an outburst.

Bob was filled with fear and anxiety about the idea of going into his own bed. We did a Bedtime Plan with the help of a child psychologist and a speech therapist. We did lots of work on trying to get Bob to recognize anxious feelings and learn to deal with them. We also came up with ideas to help Bob to fall asleep.

We didn't just say 'Right Bob, you've got to sleep in your own bed from now on'. It took weeks of work to do the preparation. Everything had to be broken down, looked at, thought through and planned. We always thought we had a routine for Bob before bed but when we looked closely, we hadn't. This is another example of how you need to look at everything and everyone when trying to resolve a problem that on first inspection looks as though it is related only to the child with Asperger Sydrome (AS).

Creating a strict pre-bedtime and bedtime routine was an essential part of the Bedtime Plan and we continue to use routine at bedtime though we are able to be a bit more flexible these days. Bob was involved every step of the way and he worked really hard at the meetings with the professionals and at home with us.

Because a lot of the work was done over a period of weeks with the professionals it would be too difficult to record it all here. We include this example to show how, with enough thought and planning, you can overcome even very big challenges with your child. We had help with the build-up to the plan, helping Bob to recognize and deal with his anxiety, which was really useful, but we devised the actual Bedtime Plan and its rewards ourselves.

We designed a programme to record Bob's progress and to reward Bob for sleeping in his own bed. We wrote some scripts to help Bob to understand why he should be sleeping in his own bed. We have included these as an example of how scripts and the reward plan can work together.

The Bedtime Plan is the most daunting thing we have done with Bob because it needed careful handling and we are very grateful for the support we got from the professionals. If you are not currently receiving any support for your child and would like to look into support opportunities then please see the chapter on useful resources at the end of the book.

The Bedtime Plan was very successful and now Bob says he can hardly remember a time when he wasn't sleeping in his own bed! We started the Bedtime Plan with lots of rewards and incentives and gradually reduced these as Bob got more and more confident at sleeping in his own bed.

Below are the original Bedtime Plan and subsequent revised versions, the scripts we used and an example of the star chart we designed. We have also included the diagram that showed Bob how to recognise feelings in his body that could be signs of anxiety.

Notice how carefully we have worded the Bedtime Plan. If there is room for ambiguity, or if a certain eventuality is not accounted for, your child with AS will find it!

The original Bedtime Plan

How Bob's Bedtime Plan will work:

If Bob spends part of the night in his own bed he will get a red star for his chart and a sticker for his sticker book to say 'well done for trying'.

If Bob spends most of the night in his own bed he will get a blue star for his star chart and three stickers for his sticker book to say 'well done for trying'.

If Bob spends the whole night in his bed he will get a gold star for his star chart and four stickers for his sticker book. Bob will also get a small reward the following morning such as a bar of chocolate, a new comic or a pound to spend. He will also get ten points for his Reward Plan.

At the end of the week we will look at the stars on the chart.

MOSTLY GOLD STARS = A BIG REWARD.

MOSTLY BLUE STARS = A MEDIUM REWARD.

MOSTLY RED STARS = A SMALL REWARD.

If no colour star dominates the chart then Dad and Mum will decide on the reward.

REWARDS:

SMALL REWARD =   A bar of chocolate

                   or

                   A comic

                   or

                   A pound coin.

MEDIUM REWARD = Something from the
                   reward bag, a toy or game.

BIG REWARD =   Something Bob really
                           wants, maybe a book or an
                           audio book on CD or tape,
                           or a toy.

The Bedtime Plan will begin on January 24th and be reviewed on February 21st.

Example of bedtime star chart

Week One	Week Two	Week Three	Week Four
Monday ★	Monday	Monday	Monday
Tuesday ★	Tuesday	Tuesday	Tuesday
Wednesday ☆	Wednesday	Wednesday	Wednesday
Thursday ★	Thursday	Thursday	Thursday
Friday ★	Friday	Friday	Friday
Saturday ★	Saturday	Saturday	Saturday
Sunday ★	Sunday	Sunday	Sunday

☆ (red star) = I spent part of the night in my own bed.

★ (blue star) = I spent most of the night in my own bed.

★ (gold star) = I spent the whole night in my own bed.

Example

WEEK ONE – Mostly Gold Stars which means I get a big
              reward at the end of the week.

Worried/Anxious feelings

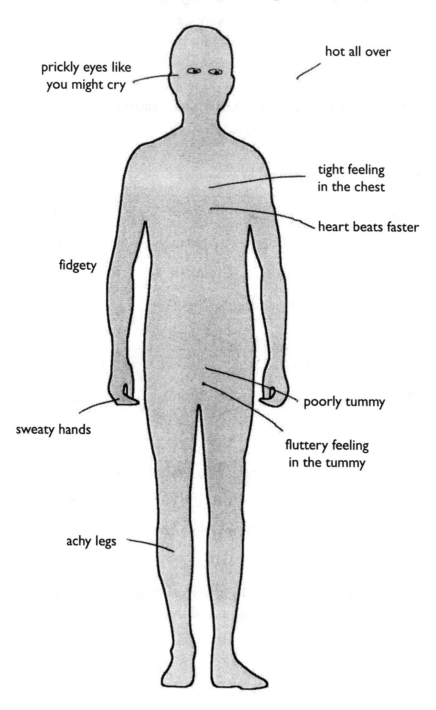

prickly eyes like
you might cry

hot all over

tight feeling
in the chest

heart beats faster

fidgety

poorly tummy

sweaty hands

fluttery feeling
in the tummy

achy legs

Three scripts for the Bedtime Plan

Learning to sleep in my own bed

Most children who are my age or older sleep in their own bed. Mum and Dad will be really pleased if I try to learn to sleep in my own bed.

I might find it difficult to learn to sleep in my own bed. I might feel really worried or scared about sleeping in my own bed. Christine [the psychologist] and Alison [the speech therapist] have some good ideas for helping children learn to sleep in their own beds. Christine and Alison know that I might feel worried or scared. They have some good ideas for helping children to feel less worried or scared. They will probably be able to help me learn to feel less worried or scared sleeping in my bed.

Sleep – why is it good for me to sleep?

When I go to sleep my whole body has a chance to rest.

Sleep also gives my mind a rest. When I have a good night's sleep I wake up feeling refreshed.

When I have enough sleep I feel happy. I have enough energy and enthusiasm for the day ahead.

Sleep is good for other people too. It is good for their body and their mind.

Sleep is good for their health and their happiness.

Lack of sleep and how it affects me

If I do not get enough sleep I will feel tired the next day.

When I am tired I feel grumpy.

If I do not get enough sleep I will get upset more easily.

If I do not get enough sleep I will not enjoy my day as much as I would like to.

Everyone needs to have a good night's sleep.

Lack of sleep makes people feel tired, upset and even ill.

A tired person will be irritable and not much fun to have around.

It is very important that everyone in my family has enough sleep.

Bedtime Plan reviews

February 21st

Bob has now been sleeping in his own bed for one month. Apart from the first night Bob has achieved a gold star every night. It is now time to move on to the next stage of the Bedtime Plan. This means that Mum will have some time downstairs while Bob is falling asleep.

★ Lights out at 8.45 pm.

★ At 9 pm Mum will check briefly on Bob. Mum will not be having a conversation with Bob but will just pop into the room to see that everything is okay.

★ At 9.15 pm Mum will come upstairs and remain upstairs until Bob is asleep.

★ If Bob stays in bed, without shouting down to Mum, between 8.45 pm and 9.15 pm Bob will get two extra stickers the next day. This also includes not keeping Mum talking when Mum checks on Bob at 9 pm.

★ All stars, next morning rewards and end of week rewards will remain the same at present.

★ The next review will be on March 7th.

March 7th

Bob has now been sleeping in his own bed for about six weeks. For the past two weeks Mum has had from 8.45 pm to 9.15 pm downstairs, checking on Bob at 9 pm. Bob hasn't shouted down at all in this time! Bob has continued to achieve a gold star every night.

From March 7th we will continue with the bedtime routine except that Mum will go to bed at 9.30 pm instead of 9.15 pm. If Bob doesn't shout down in this time he can have four extra stickers the next morning, a total of eight stickers.

★ All other points and next day rewards and end of week rewards will remain the same.

★ The Bedtime Plan will be reviewed again on March 20th.

March 20th

Bob has continued to sleep in his own bed and hasn't shouted down to Mum or kept Mum talking at the 9 pm check. Bob has achieved a great deal and we are very proud of him. From March 21st Bob will remain in bed while Mum stays downstairs until 9.45 pm.

★ Mum or Dad will continue to check on Bob at 9 pm. and then Mum will not come to bed until 9.45 pm.

★ All rewards, points and end of week rewards will remain the same.

★ The Bedtime Plan will be reviewed in two weeks on April 3rd.

April 3rd

Bob has continued to achieve a gold star every night.

★ Mum will now come to bed at 10 pm.

★ All rewards and the 9 pm check will remain the same.

★ The Bedtime Plan will be reviewed on April 17th.

April 17th

Bob has continued to achieve gold stars and should be very proud of himself.

★ From April 18th Mum can now come to bed at whatever time she likes!

★ Dad or Mum will continue to check on Bob at 9 pm.

★ Bob must not keep Mum talking or shout down to Mum.

★ All rewards will remain the same for now.

May 2nd

Bob is now doing so well with his Bedtime Plan that it is now time to reduce his rewards, gradually. From today Bob will not get stickers each morning. He can now keep his sticker books and stickers and use them whenever he likes.

From May 9th Bob's next day rewards will start to be phased out. He will be able to get a reward each day until the bag is empty.

The 10 points, gold star and gold star reward at the end of the week will remain.

May 26th

Because Bob is so good at sleeping in his own bed it is now time to reduce the number of points Bob gets for this.

★ From May 30th Bob will now get 5 points for sleeping in his own bed.

★ Bob will be able to get extra points at bedtime by doing the following things:

   ☆ Not shouting Mum if Mum has come to bed while Bob is still awake.

   ☆ Taking himself to the toilet and putting himself back into bed. Mum and Dad will help Bob learn how to do this and give him some practice.

Eventually all points and rewards were gradually phased out and Bob continues to sleep in his own bed. Sometimes he shouts down to Mum and we remind him of the skills he learned about coping with anxious feelings. Bob sometimes puts himself back into bed after getting up for the toilet but still sometimes shouts for Mum. We are using the reward plan to help Bob become more independent in this area.

Bob's comments on the Bedtime Plan

The Bedtime Plan helped because it gave me something to work towards. It was good to get lots of rewards for all my hard work.

The 'Caring for myself tasks' Plan

This is the second 'big' reward plan that we did with Bob. It became necessary because Bob was and still is completely uninterested in his appearance. There are lots of things Bob does care about. He loves to read and collects books, especially by particular authors. He loves and collects dragons, he loves nature and has recently 'got into' films and computer games. Bob has always written beautiful poetry and has recently started writing two fantasy/action-type books. He particularly loves his two dogs. So, as you can see, Bob has lots of interests but he has absolutely no interest in his appearance.

Bob ridicules fashion and thinks clothes only need to be comfortable (not necessarily clean, just comfortable!). He has always hated getting washed, washing his hair, trying on new clothes, anything connected to his appearance really. We think this is partly due to his skin sensitivity, which is common for people with autism. Also, probably due to AS, Bob is concerned with his immediate needs and satisfying those. He doesn't concern himself with what other people think about him. He is not interested in doing something just because his peers are doing it. He has no interest in keeping up with clothes or music fashion. He likes what he likes. We think these are very positive aspects of AS but they do present some challenges, especially when it comes to personal care.

Bob's puberty began at the age of ten. Although Bob is very mature intellectually he is very young emotionally and he was in no way ready to start growing up. Unfortunately for Bob his puberty has been rapid. Particularly noticeable were his emerging body odour and his spots!

Puberty is a difficult and confusing time for any child but often, along with the anxiety, there is an excitement about growing up, comparing development with peers, and interest in the opposite or same sex as a potential boyfriend or girlfriend. Bob doesn't experience any of this and he is very anxious about growing up.

We needed to make a plan to help Bob with his progressing puberty and to help him to understand the physical and social impact that caring or not caring for himself properly would have. This time we did the reward plan, scripts and reward chart as a family, without any input from professionals. We made some mistakes and had to adapt the plan a few times but we have included the mistakes in this book so that you can see the process. As with all the changes we expect Bob to make, we had to make our own changes and there had to be a lot of incentives for Bob.

Below are the scripts we wrote for each aspect of Bob's personal care and the charts we designed to record Bob's progress (pp.89–97).

A few months into the plan, Bob is no longer filling in the charts. He is just getting on with his 'Caring for myself tasks' each day. Bob doesn't always remember to do them all and still needs reminders and help with some of them but he is prepared to do them and rarely complains.

As with the Bedtime Plan we will gradually reduce the rewards as caring for himself will, we hope, become second nature. This is quite a way off in the future but Bob has proved to us that he can achieve what he wants to achieve. We have every confidence in Bob!

DAY	Teeth x 3	Cleansing x 2	Medicine x 2
Monday			
Tuesday			
Wednesday			
Thursday			
Friday			
Saturday			
Sunday			
Do I get my end of week 'big' reward?			

✓ = REWARD   O = No REWARD

Bob's 'Caring for myself tasks' plan

	MONDAY	TUESDAY	WEDNESDAY	THURSDAY	FRIDAY	SATURDAY	SUNDAY
Morning	Clean clothes and socks.	Clean clothes and socks.	Clean clothes and socks.	Clean clothes and socks.	Clean clothes and socks. *	Clean clothes and socks.	Clean clothes and socks.
Afternoon							
Evening			Bath or shower. Wash body thoroughly.		If I have a shower and wash my hair after swimming I don't need to wash my hair on Friday.		Bath or shower. Hair washed. Wash body thoroughly. Nails cut.

Bob's 'Caring for myself tasks' chart

The initial script to introduce the 'Caring for myself tasks' Plan

Every day I need to:

   take my medicine twice,

   brush my teeth twice,

   cleanse my nose twice,

   put cream or lotion on my spots twice.

   I also need to get a bath or shower at least twice a week.

   I need to wash my hair once a week.

   I need clean clothes, including socks, at least every other day.

   If Mum or Dad think my clothes need changing more often then I must change them even if I haven't had them on for long.

   I also need my nails checking and cutting once a week.

Dad and Mum will make charts to record what needs doing, when and how often.

   I will do these 'Caring for myself tasks' when Dad or Mum ask and if I do them calmly I will get a star for each thing each time I do it.

   If I get all my stars for the day I will get a small reward at the end of each day.

   If I get all of my stars for the week I will get a bigger reward every Sunday.

   Dad and Mum know that I don't like doing some of my 'Caring for myself tasks'. Dad and Mum try hard to understand that it is hard for me to cleanse my skin, for example, because it stings. This is why Dad and Mum are going to reward me for doing my 'Caring for myself tasks'.

I will try to understand how important my 'Caring for myself tasks' are and will learn more about them and about puberty with Dad and Mum.

Separate scripts to support the 'Caring for myself tasks' Plan

Brushing my teeth

I have agreed to brush my teeth at least three times a day.

If I have food stuck in my teeth or my teeth just don't look clean then I have agreed to brush my teeth more often, whenever Dad or Mum ask me to, or if I see food stuck in my teeth or I notice that my teeth don't look clean.

It is very important to keep my teeth and gums healthy.

If I don't look after my teeth I will get tooth decay and gum disease.

If I get tooth decay or gum disease I will experience pain and I may lose some of my teeth.

I need my teeth to eat and to help me to pronounce my words properly.

I also need to look after my teeth for social reasons.

If my breath smells bad then people will not want me to stand close to them or talk to them.

I could lose friends if I have smelly breath.

I also need clean teeth because teeth that are dirty or have food stuck in them look horrible and will put people off talking to me or being my friend.

At the moment I am taking very good care of my teeth and the dentist is always pleased with me!

Baths and showers

I have agreed to get a bath or shower at least twice a week.

This is the minimum and Dad or Mum may ask me to have a bath or shower more often than this.

When I am older I will need to have a bath or shower every other day, then every day. Dad and Mum will decide when this is.

When I have my bath or shower I need to put lots of soap on my sponge and wash very thoroughly, especially under my arms and around my genitals. These areas can get very smelly and I don't want to get an infection.

When I have a bath or shower I must also wash my hair.

I must put lots of shampoo on, scrub and rinse thoroughly, otherwise my head and hair will smell.

I must keep myself clean because I don't want to get poorly with infections.

I also need to keep clean for social reasons.

People who don't wash regularly and thoroughly get body odour. Body odour smells horrible and puts people off you.

If I get body odour it will be hard to keep friends let alone make new ones.

I am getting good at washing my body and my hair.

I am getting good at taking care of myself.

Dad and Mum are very pleased with how well I am taking care of myself.

Cleansing my skin

My hormones are changing, preparing my body for puberty.

Because of this I am experiencing changes in my skin.

I am getting lots of spots around my nose and chin.

Sometimes these spots can be sore and if I don't cleanse them thoroughly and deeply they will become infected, spread and cause me pain.

I have agreed to cleanse my nose morning and night to help to clear away spots and stop spots from getting infected. Sometimes I cleanse my own skin but at least once a day Dad or Mum will cleanse my skin for me just to make sure of a thorough cleanse until I am more practised at it.

I have also agreed to have spot lotion on twice a day, to be applied after the cleansing.

It is important to cleanse my skin for health reasons but also for social reasons. If I have very spotty, red, infected skin it will not look nice and will put people off being close to me and maybe even put people off being my friend.

I have friends who think a lot of me, they like my personality so hopefully they wouldn't go off me but it may be hard to make new friends if my face is full of pus.

People shouldn't judge us by appearance but many of them do.

At the moment I am taking very good care of my skin by cleansing twice a day and using spot cream twice a day.

Dad and Mum are very pleased with me.

Having my nails cleaned and cut

It is important to keep my nails clean.

It is important to have my nails cut.

As I often put my fingers in my mouth when eating then I need to keep my nails clean to protect myself from germs.

I also need to keep my nails cut because if they get too long I could scratch myself or someone else by accident.

I need to keep my nails cut for social reasons.

If I have grubby nails it will not look nice and people may think that I do not wash properly.

It is hard to keep friends or make new ones if a person doesn't look clean.

I will try hard to keep my nails fairly clean and well cut.

Changing my clothes

Everybody must change their clothes regularly if they are able to.

I have lots of clothes and am able to change them regularly.

If I don't change my clothes when they need changing then my clothes will begin to smell.

If my clothes are smelly it will be hard for me to keep my friends or to make new ones.

Body odour is very offensive and most people will not be prepared to put up with it.

I will know that my clothes need changing if they get dirt or food stains on.

Sometimes the dirt will be invisible but smelly, like sweat.

If my clothes look or smell dirty I must change them.

It is best to change my clothes, including socks, at least every other day.

I may need to change my clothes more often than this if they are stained or smelly.

Mum and Dad will be very pleased if I change my clothes when asked to.

Mum and Dad will be even more pleased if I learn to recognize when my clothes need changing.

The following script became necessary because Bob was either being aggressive when doing his 'Caring for myself tasks' or messing about and wasting a lot of time so that each task was becoming quite stressful. Using this script helped him to calm down and take the tasks seriously. He got points on his reward chart for being calm and gentle during these tasks.

Keeping calm before, during and after my 'Caring for myself tasks'

When Dad or Mum asks me to do a 'Caring for myself task' I must do it as soon as I am asked.

On the way to the bathroom I must stay calm and treat Mum and Dad gently and with respect.

Whilst in the bathroom I must remain calm and gentle and not 'mess about' (for example, I must not dance around).

I must have my 'Caring for myself task' done straight away and not cause a delay (for example, I must not pick the dog up).

If I am annoyed at Dad or Mum or worried or concerned about anything during this time I must try to tell them calmly. (For example, needing to close my eyes before Mum or Dad do my teeth.)

To earn my star I must be calm, gentle and respectful before my task, on the way to my task, during my task and on the way from my task.

If I am calm and gentle before, during and after my 'Caring for myself' tasks then Dad and Mum will be very pleased with me and I will be pleased with myself.

Bob's comments on the 'Caring for myself tasks' Plan

I think that this plan has probably helped me to learn to look after myself better. I like this plan because it earns me money to buy things for myself.

What else might you create a specific reward plan for?

A reward plan could help your child with AS to adapt his or her behaviour in many different areas of life. What you choose to base your plan on will depend on what your child finds challenging. Consider and discuss with your child which situations are regularly causing anxiety or which tasks he or she lacks confidence in performing. These could be:

★ following a morning routine of getting dressed independently

★ travelling on a bus or train

★ visiting other family members or friends

★ being flexible about the scheduling of routines

★ learning to get changed at the swimming baths independently (we recently did this with Bob)

★ going into a shop independently and asking for/purchasing something

★ caring for a pet

★ any aspect of your child's development that involves assessing and planning how to handle 'risk', such as crossing the road

★ preparing for a situation where your child needs to spend time away from you, such as attending a club

★ going into any social situation that your child finds difficult.

Chapter 7

Conclusion

We hope that this book has been of some use to you. Bob's Asperger Syndrome (AS) is changing and growing almost as quickly as he is. We are finding that we are having to change and grow too, to keep up with him. This includes changing and adapting the techniques we use. It seems that Bob and his AS are a 'work in progress'.

In the process of writing this book things have changed a great deal. Bob is now more able to tell us what works for him and why. He has recently started to say that we should ask him for advice on coping with the challenges that AS brings and we are trying to do this and trying to listen to him and act on what he says. We believe that the techniques we have used so far, especially the reward plan, have helped Bob and us to get to this point.

Things are still very challenging for us and for Bob. There is no 'quick fix' to the down sides of AS. It takes a lot of hard work and cooperation from everyone in the family, sometimes, just to get through the day!

Looking after yourselves as parents

We have only touched briefly on parents' or guardians' feelings in all this and about how important it is to look after yourself. Using the techniques we recommend can take a lot of time, commitment and energy. We can't emphasize enough how important it is to take care of yourself and to be selfish sometimes. We have not been very good at this and it has begun to tell on our health at times.

We are trying really hard to take some time out for ourselves now and when we do the whole family feels the benefit. Bob's mum knows that she is far more patient with Bob when she has had a break and so the techniques we use are more likely to be successful if we have the energy and the patience to do them (sometimes we don't have the energy and we soon feel things slipping). Only you know what you like to do and what helps you to relax so please try to make the time and do it. Here are some suggestions:

★ have a relaxing bath

★ go for a walk

★ visit a friend

★ go out for a meal

★ watch a film

★ relax with a book

★ go to the theatre

★ spend time on your own special interest if you have one, e.g. yoga or playing an instrument – whatever takes your mind off the matters of daily life

★ if you are part of a couple, take time out to spend together, child-free

★ spend time on yourself, for example have a haircut or go on a personal shopping trip where you make sure you don't come back with anything for the child/children, just for yourself.

Each day we do Bob's home education, his physiotherapy and occupational therapy exercises, work from his psychologist and speech therapist around his social and communication skills and his emotions – and all this before the more day-to-day stuff of just being parents! No, we are not superparents, and yes, it does all get a bit much sometimes, especially for Bob. We try to have at least one day a week where we do none of this, except the points for his reward plan as he would hate to miss out on these!

No one is perfect and you will never achieve all you want to achieve because you are human and not superhuman. Remember that you can only do as much as you can do for your child and please try not to feel guilty or despondent too often.

If you think that our reward plan and our supplementary techniques will help your child then please use them. We hope that you will find them as helpful as we do.

So, from Bob, his mum and his dad, goodbye, good luck and take care!

Chapter 8

Useful Resources

Here we list some resources that we hope you will find helpful. There is such a wealth of information now about Asperger Syndrome (AS) and autism in general but sometimes it is hard to know where to start to get the information you're looking for. Some of these websites may be a good starting point as many of them have links to other useful sites as well.

Resources relating to AS and autism
United Kingdom
The National Autistic Society (NAS)
393 City Road
London
EC1V 1NG
Tel. +44(0) 20 7833 2299
Email nas@nas.org.uk

The National Autistic Society offers lots of advice and support to people with an autistic spectrum disorder and to people who are affected by autism, such as relatives and friends. We have found the NAS to be very helpful. Their website is full of advice and news and has many links to other useful resources.

Canada

Autism Society Canada
Box 22017
1670 Heron Road
Ottawa
Ontario
K1V OC2
Email info@autismsocietycanada.ca

Founded in 1976, the Autism Society Canada aims to support people in Canada who are affected by autism. The ASC provides information about autistic spectrum disorders in general, advocacy, and education, and has links to other helpful services and resources.

USA

Autism Society of America (ASA)
7910 Woodmont Avenue, Suite 300
Bethesda
Maryland
20814-3067
USA
Tel. (+1) 301.657.0881 or (+1) 1.800.3AUTISM
(1.800.328.8476)
www.autism-society.org

Founded by Bernard Rimland, the ASA is a huge organization offering information about autism spectrum disorders, how and where to get help across the USA, education and treatment options and much more.

OASIS (Online Asperger Syndrome Information and Support)
www.aspergersyndrome.org
Email bkirby@udel.edu

This site has information on lots of issues relating to AS, including social skills, and also related disorders, as well as links to AS support in many other countries such as France and India. It was set up by parents but has grown and is now a widely used resource.

Australia

Asperger Syndrome Australian Information Centre
http://members.ozemail.com.au/~rbmitch/Asperger.htm
Email rbmitch@ozemail.com.au

This site has many useful links. It also contains information and advice about AS in general, education, support groups and other useful topics relating to AS. The site was founded and is run by parents.

Tony Attwood
The Asperger Syndrome Clinic
P.O. Box 224
Petrie
Queensland 4502
Australia
Tel. (61) 7 3285 7888
www.tonyattwood.com.au
Email tony@tonyattwood.com.au

Tony Attwood is an expert in AS. We have attended one of his presentations about AS and found it very informative. His personal assistant Dawn Sheahan can be contacted by email or phone.

Resources relating to home education

Many children with AS and other autistic spectrum disorders find school an overwhelming and traumatic experience. Often these children are bullied and almost always mainstream schools are unable to meet the specific needs of autistic children. Parents often find themselves battling with the school to secure the support that should be an automatic right for these children. Some children with autism go through their whole school career feeling stressed, ignored and depressed. Parents long for an alternative but most parents don't know that there actually is an alternative, home education!

The rules surrounding home education are different in each country. If you are considering home education for your child then the following websites may give you a useful insight into the home education situation where you live.

Home education isn't just for children with specific needs. It is a real option for all children. We know lots of families who home educate as a life choice and have very happy children who have never been to school!

UK and Ireland

Education Otherwise
PO Box 325
Kings Lynn
PE34 3XW
www.educationotherwise.org
Email webmaster@education-otherwise.org or
eoemailhelpline@education-otherwise.org

We are members of Education Otherwise and have found them to be very helpful and supportive. Like many charities it started out with a group of parents trying to support each other and grew from there. EO can offer advice and support to families home-educating in England, Ireland, Scotland and Wales but they do have members living in other parts of the world. It is named so because the law in England states that parents have to provide a suitable education for their children at school or otherwise and more and more parents are choosing 'otherwise'!

HEN Ireland (Home Education Network)
www.henireland.org
Email kimpierce@eircom.net

This website was set up by parents to support each other in home education. It has a contact list to put members in touch with each other, a section for teenagers and one for younger children, a library and information about the legal aspects of home educating in Ireland.

Other countries

About.com: Homeschooling
http://homeschooling.about.com/cs

This site has links about home education in lots of different countries including Australia, New Zealand, Canada and the USA.

A to Z Home's Cool
http://homeschooling.gomilpitas.com
Email homeschoolguide@gomilpitas.com

This site has links about home education in lots of different countries. It has a wealth of information including the legal aspects of home educating around the world.

Joyfully Rejoycing (Joyce Fetteroll – USA)
www.joyfullyrejoycing.com

This is a lovely website about the joys of home education and about peaceful parenting, for example, alternatives to smacking.

We hope that you find some of the above resources useful in your search for information regarding autism and AS and, for those of you who may be interested in home education, remember that no one cares about your child as much as you do so if you choose to home educate you won't be letting your child down, you will be giving them room to grow into the person they were meant to be.

Advice on and resources for financial help
Funding the reward plan

When you are using the reward plan you have to think carefully about how much you are prepared to, or how much you can afford to spend on rewards for your child. We have included some ideas for rewards that don't cost money in Chapter 3. However, when you have a child with additional needs then costs will invariably rise.

As we live in the UK, we were able to apply for and subsequently claim Disability Living Allowance. We use Bob's Disability Living Allowance to fund the reward plan. The benefit system will be different for different countries so below we have listed some organizations that may be able to offer help and advice on claiming benefits, awards or grants in different parts of the world.

As we emphasized in Chapter 3, charity shops can be very useful and inexpensive places for picking up toys and books that your child may want. You can also offer rewards that don't cost money, such as extra computer time or staying up late.

We want reward plans to be accessible to all children with AS or autism and so the more creative you can be with ideas for rewards the easier the plan will be to afford and implement. However, you may want to buy things to reward your child with. The sites below may help you to gain some financial help toward your child's reward plan.

Some general advice on getting financial help for your child with autism: care and mobility

If your child needs more help and support to care for him- or herself than a neurotypical child of the same age then they may be entitled to some level of financial help from the government or a charity. Of course this will vary from country to country and so this is very much a general guide.

Your child may need help with dressing, feeding, bathing, brushing teeth and so on. We think this should mean not only can your child do these tasks independently but also with no problems. If your child gets distressed doing these things and has outbursts similar to the ones Bob used to have before embarking on his 'Caring for myself tasks' Plan then his or her care needs are above and beyond those of a 'typical' child of the same age.

Or, if it takes your child ages to get dressed, even if he or she can do this independently, because they have a skin sensitivity related to autism, then we think that your child has care needs greater than those of other children of a similar age.

These are just examples, so look at every aspect of your child's physical care. Is it as straightforward for your child as for a neurotypical child of the same age or are there additional care needs? Think carefully, and write them all down.

In the UK children with autism are entitled to a financial benefit to help with their additional care needs and depending on where you live your child may also be entitled to financial help to aid their mobility. Parents often think that this means 'can your child walk without difficulty?' and often children can't. However, many children with autism can walk okay but they may 'run off' in the street, have outbursts in the street or refuse to walk altogether. We would class this as a mobility need because it puts the child and adult at risk when out and about. Your child is just as likely to need access to a car or taxi as a physically disabled child. Bob often forgets to stop at the kerb and isn't at a stage yet where he goes out alone as most of his neurotypical friends do.

Applying for a benefit/grant

When you are applying for a benefit or grant for your child take some time to observe your child and maybe even keep a diary. Write down all the things you notice that your child needs help with that a neurotypical child of the same age could probably do without too many problems.

Write down all the questions you want to ask whoever you are applying to. Write down everything you want to tell them. Take a photocopy of any forms you fill in for future reference. You may want to get help or advice on filling in the form from a person who specializes in helping with welfare or benefit claims.

Applying for a benefit or grant or any other form of financial help can be daunting and sometimes feel degrading. This is unfair as you and your child are entitled to this money and it can be humiliating having to divulge personal information about yourself and your child. This often puts people off applying for things that they should have an automatic right to.

We didn't apply for any benefits for Bob for a long time for this very reason. We still haven't applied for all that we know we are entitled to. Bob's mum didn't want to apply for any financial help for Bob because of a fear of having all this personal information about Bob written down somewhere. Bob's dad helps people to claim benefits as part of his job as a mental health social worker and so knew exactly how to get the best result. Most parents are not in this fortunate position.

If you need extra help for your child and you can overcome the anxiety of applying for help then try to get advice before you go ahead. You will stand more chance of receiving the money and of having some control over the situation if you take your time and plan your application carefully.

Good luck with accessing the financial help that you and your child deserve! The following websites may be of use.

Patient Centered Guides – Autism Center
www.oreilly.com/medical/autism/news/financial.html

Under 'Direct and Indirect financial support for families' you can access information regarding possible financial support for the following countries: the USA, Canada, the UK, Ireland, Australia and New Zealand.

Autism Recovery Information – Australia
www.autismrecovery.org.au
Email blog@autismrecovery.com.au

This site offers information about claiming Family Tax from the Family Assistance Office and about claiming 'Carer's

Allowance'. There is lots of information about autism in general on this site also.

The Autism Society of America (see p.104 above) also has links to sites that give information about accessing financial awards for people with autism.